Comprehension

John Butterworth

Illustrations by Lee Nicholls

428

OXFORD
UNIVERSITY PRESS

OXFORD
UNIVERSITY PRESS

Great Clarendon Street, Oxford OX2 6DP

Oxford University Press is a department of the University of Oxford.
It furthers the University's objective of excellence in research, scholarship,
and education by publishing worldwide in

Oxford New York

Auckland Bangkok Buenos Aires
Cape Town Chennai Dar es Salaam Delhi Hong Kong Istanbul
Karachi Kolkata Kuala Lumpur Madrid Melbourne Mexico City Mumbai
Nairobi São Paulo Shanghai Taipei Tokyo Toronto

Oxford is a registered trade mark of Oxford University Press
in the UK and in certain other countries

British Library Cataloguing in Publication Data available

ISBN 0–19–911162–6

1 3 5 7 9 10 8 6 4 2

Designed and Typeset by Mike Brain Graphic Design Limited
Printed in Hong Kong

Acknowledgements

The editors and publishers gratefully acknowledge permission to reproduce the following
copyright material:
'Wind' from *Hawk in the Rain*, by Ted Hughes copyright © 1957. Reprinted by permission
of Faber and Faber Ltd.
Covers by Quentin Blake for *Danny the Champion of the World* and *Boy: Tales of Childhood*
by Roald Dahl (Puffin, 2000) Illustrations © Quentin Blake, 2000. Reprinted by permission of
Penguin Books Ltd.

Contents

What is a Text?   4

Kinds of Text   6

Fact or Fiction   8

Reading a Story   10

Who, What, Where, Why... ?   12

Dialogue   14

On with the Plot   16

On Stage and Screen   18

Hitting the Headlines   20

What's What   22

Fact or Opinion   23

For Information and Reference   24

Not Literally   26

Poetry   28

Index   30

Kate

Tom

Jas

Bee

Look in the Index on pages 30–32 for more information on a key comprehension term when you see this.

What is a Text?

A **text** can be anything that is written or spoken out loud.
Texts can be as short as a few words, or as long as a whole book.

Texts have all sorts of different **purposes**. Some give information.
Some give warnings or instructions. Others tell stories. Others
describe people, places, or things.

Here are several short
pieces of text. What do
you think the purpose
of each one is?

B

DITCHFORD DANCE FESTIVAL

Town Hall Theatre
Friday 24 March
7.30 p.m.
Tickets from £6.00

A
Hi, I'm Tom. Every Saturday I play football. Then I go down to the café to meet my mates. There are four of us: Kate who rides horses and wants to be a jockey. Bee who does dancing lessons. She's really good. And Jas, well, Jas just talks a lot...

C
Learn to ride at Angie's Riding School
Expert instruction. Horses and ponies to suit all ages. Free-trial lesson for beginners.

E
SCOFFALOTTI'S
Special All Day Breakfast
☆
A giant's feast of crispy bacon, sausages, hash-browns, eggs, beans, and tomato, with a steaming mug of tea or coffee
£3.75

D
Scene 1: INSIDE *SCOFFALOTTI'S* CAFÉ.
MARIO, THE WAITER, IS SERVING DRINKS IN CANS TO FOUR YOUNG PEOPLE SITTING AT ONE OF THE TABLES. THEY ARE LAUGHING AT SOMETHING ONE OF THEM HAS SAID. A WELL-DRESSED MAN AND WOMAN, SITTING AT THE NEXT TABLE, ARE NOT AMUSED.

F

Kate Sampson

Date of birth 5/6/90

Address: 21 Eastway, Ditchford.

Sisters 1, brothers 2

Interests: Horse-riding, swimming, and reading

G

Jas's work has been better this term. His reading and comprehension have really improved. Unfortunately, he is still too talkative in class, and often distracts others with his chatter...

H

ARMED RAID ON DITCHFORD POST OFFICE

Siân Field reports

Masked thieves held up a local post office earlier today, and escaped with thousands of pounds worth of cash and postal orders...

I

◆ CHAPTER 1 ◆

Beatrice was as changeable as the weather. One moment she'd be sulking, the next she'd be bubbling with excitement. It was no wonder she liked dancing: skipping round the room, never still for a second. She changed her clothes about ten times a day, and her mind every five minutes. 'Blowing in the breeze' her mother called it.

7

Kinds of Text

As you saw on pages 4 and 5, there are many different kinds of text, written for different reasons and for different people.

The skill of understanding these different types of text is called **comprehension**. Think of comprehension as being like a treasure hunt. Texts contain a trail of clues that lead you to their full meaning.

Instructions

For example, this text gives **instructions**, telling the reader or listener how to do something. It is probably meant for people who are interested in learning to ride a horse.

- Stand with your left side to the horse's left side and take hold of the reins and saddle.
- Put your left foot into the stirrup and spring up, swinging your right leg over the saddle.
- Sit down.

How do we know these are instructions? The answer is that the text gives us clues. One of the clues here is that the sentences are written as commands:

take hold of the reins… spring up….

Information

Though it stays on the subject of horses, the next piece is a completely different kind of text. It doesn't give instructions, it gives facts.

A horse is an intelligent and sensitive animal. It knows immediately if the person trying to get on its back is an experienced rider, or a beginner. People who know what they're doing make a horse feel safe; people who don't make a horse feel nervous, and that is when they misbehave.

Texts like this give **information**, describe things, investigate them, or explain them. One clue is that the sentences are in the present tense:
A horse is an intelligent animal.   …that is when they misbehave.

Narrative

Here is another kind of text. How is it different from the instructions and the information text?

> Kate slipped her left foot into the stirrup. With the reins in her hand, she swung her leg up and over, and dropped lightly into the saddle. Kate had been riding since she was six, and she knew all about horses.
>
> *45*

This is written in the way a story would be told. It is about a **character** – *Kate* – and the sentences are about what *she did*. The name for this kind of text is **narrative**.

Narrative can be written in the *past tense*, or in the *present tense*. This piece is in the past tense. If it had been in the present tense, the first sentence would have been:

Kate <u>slips</u> her left foot into the stirrup.

The next example is also a piece of narrative, but it sounds quite different.

> *Wednesday May 21* – Kate got me to go riding. Must have been mad to agree. Fell off three times – Kate says that's good luck. I'm having to write this standing up. Guess why!!!
>
> *Saturday May 24* – Me, Kate, Bee, and Tom met at Scoff's like we always do. Something really weird happened...

What makes this narrative different is that it is written in the **first person**: the writer is *I* or *me*. It is not about *he*, *she*, *him*, *her*, or *Kate* as above. That narrative is written in the **third person**.

This text could be from a diary or from a story written to sound like a diary. Who might be the audience for this diary text?

The person or people that a text is written for are called the **audience,** whether they are readers or listeners. Often you can tell just by looking at a text what sort of audience it was meant for. Describe the audience you think the instruction text on page 6 was written for.

Fact or Fiction

If a story, or the characters in it, are made up by a writer, it's called *fiction*.

Book-length texts that are fictional are known as **novels**. Shorter pieces of fiction are just called **short stories**.

Not all stories are *fictional*, though. Some are *factual*. If you read a story in the newspaper, you expect it to be true, not made up. It's the same if you read a biography or an autobiography.

An **autobiography** is the story of somebody's life, written by themselves (in the first person).

A **biography** is the story of somebody's life, which is written by another writer (in the third person).

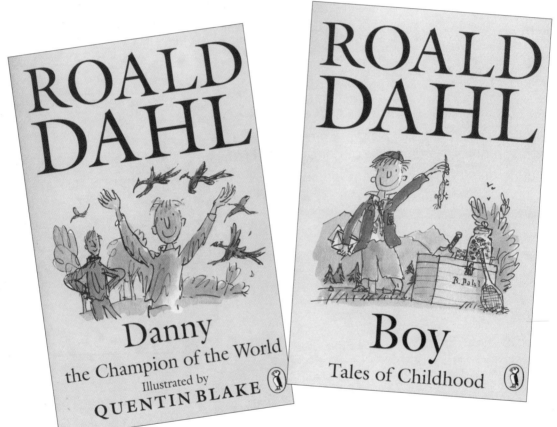

Some writers mix fact with fiction, to make a story seem real. They might use real people and make up the events. Or they might use real events and places – like London during the war – but invent the characters.

Can you think of a book or story you have read which mixes fact with fiction?

Any text that is not fiction, whether or not it's a story, is simply called *non-fiction*.

All sorts

If you go into a bookshop or a library, you will find all sorts of different labels on the shelves, showing what kinds of text you'll find there.

Fiction will be divided up into:

detective stories　　**historical fiction**
romance　　**horror**　　**science fiction**

Non-fiction will be split up into subjects, like:

gardening　　**cookery**　　**travel**　　**sport**
biography　　**music**

And books are not the only 'containers' of texts. Magazines, newspapers, noticeboards, web-sites – all contain or display texts:

stories　　**articles**　　**advertisements**
letters　　**documentaries**

Can you name the particular genre that this extract belongs to? Find three clues in the language that tell you this.

The word used for all these different kinds of text is **_genre_**. **Science fiction** is one genre. **Romance** is another. You can recognize a genre not only by the subject, but by clues in the language that is used in the text.

Once upon a time there were four friends. Rufus was a fine horse-rider, Griselda was a great warrior, Geoffrey was a clever talker, and Alison was a beautiful dancer. One winter's day a strange adventure befell them…

Reading a Story

Reading a story is like following a trail. All along the trail there are clues that help you to understand where the story is going.

The beginning of a story is particularly important. It is usually packed with clues about what is to come. If you don't pick up on them, you may find it hard to follow the rest of the story. It's like missing the beginning of a film.

Read the piece of text, which is the beginning of a story called *Lost and Found* by John Cedar. What do you think is the main clue about what is going to happen?

◆ 1 ◆

The posh-looking couple from the next table had already marched out of the café, glaring at Kate and her friends, and muttering the word 'hooligans'.

Kate, Bee, Jas, and Tom weren't really hooligans: just enjoying themselves in that special way that seems to upset adults so much. They were trying to build a pyramid out of empty drink cans, but couldn't get the last one to stay on without the whole thing collapsing.

'Right,' said the waiter, after the third tower of tins had clattered on to the tiled floor, 'it's time you lot left. Pick those up and put them on the table.' He said it in a friendly enough voice, but they knew he was a person who would stand no nonsense, and they did as they were told. 'And next Saturday, drink orange juice. The cartons don't make a noise.'

1

LOST AND FOUND

Kate crawled under the bench to get one of the cans. It was where the people who called her a hooligan had been sitting. The tin had rolled into a corner out of sight, but a sticky trail of liquid that had dribbled out led Kate straight to it.

And to something else.

On the floor, against the leg of the table was a fat brown envelope. Kate opened it and her eyes widened. Even in the gloom under the table, she could see it was stuffed with money.

Turn to pages 30–32

What the text says (and what it doesn't)

The short piece of text tells you a lot. It even contains some quite small details, like the way the drink can leaked on to the floor, and exactly what the waiter said to Kate and her friends.

But it doesn't, and it can't, tell you everything. Some things are left for you to work out for yourself.

You won't find a sentence in the opening which *says* (in so many words) that Kate and her friends are children, or that the posh-looking couple were angry. So how do you know these things? Where and what are the clues?

Working out something that isn't *said* is called **inference**. You can *infer* that the couple were angry, even though you are not told it. Comprehension involves a lot of inferring of meaning from texts.

LOST *and* FOUND

JOHN CEDAR

Words and pictures

Many stories contain clues in pictures, as well as in words. Even books with no illustrations inside usually have a picture on the cover. What information does the picture give you that the text does not in *Lost and Found*?

Who, What, Where, Why...?

To understand a story well you need to know about:
- the **characters** – *who* the story is about
- the **events** – *what* happens in the story
- the **setting** – *where* and *when* it happens

Characters

The characters of a story are the people in it. In fiction these may also be animals or toys, but they are still characters. Usually, in a story, there will be one or more *main* characters, and some other less important characters.

Of the characters you meet at the start of *Lost and Found* on page 10, which ones do you think are the main characters?

When you begin reading a story look out for clues that tell you what the characters are like, so that you can 'get to know them'. Some writers describe their characters for you. Others leave it to you to work out, or *infer*, what they are like from what they do and say.

How much are you told about the character of the waiter on page 10?
How much can you work out for yourself?

Events

Events are the things that happen in a story. The main event of *Lost and Found* so far is Kate finding the money. But don't ignore the smaller events – like the couple walking out – because they may turn out to be important later.

Always be on the lookout for *reasons* for events. They are quite often linked. For example, the couple leave because the children are knocking over the tins. And it is because one of the tins rolls under the table that Kate finds the money. So one event is the reason for another: it helps to explain *why* it happens.

Setting

Setting means the place and time of the story. The setting for the beginning of *Lost and Found* is a café. Try to imagine it, using any clues that you can find in the text or in the illustrations. For example, what are the chairs and tables like? What is the floor like? How are the walls decorated? Do you think it is an expensive café or a cheap one – and why?

Writers can choose the **voice** they tell the story in. Sometimes they choose the voice of one of the characters. Other times they use their own voice, as if they were observing events, unseen by the characters. The voice telling the story is also called the **narrator**.

The narrator chosen to tell the story can make a lot of difference to the way it is written. For example, if John Cedar had used Kate's voice to tell the story, the second paragraph might have started like this:

> Me, Bee, Jas, and Tom weren't really hooligans, just enjoying ourselves, and why not? Some people get so upset if you have a good time…

In what ways does this voice sound different from the voice used on page 10?

Dialogue

Dialogue means conversation or speech. Dialogue is very helpful in stories because it reveals a lot about the characters. Narrative tells the reader what they *do*. Dialogue tells the reader what they *say* and *how* they say it.

Here's what happens to the friends in *Lost and Found* after they leave the café.

'Look,' Kate said.

They had left the warm café and were heading for the park. They all looked at what she was holding. It didn't look like much. 'This was under the table next to us. There must be hundreds of pounds in it. Maybe thousands.'

Tom snatched the package and peered inside. He said nothing but walked on, quickly, until they came to the park gates. Then, when he was sure that no one was watching, he stopped. 'There really is,' he said. 'We're rich. Come on, let's split it.'

Bee agreed, with an excited little dance.

But Kate didn't. 'We can't do that,' she said.

'You're joking! Why not?'

'It's not ours, that's why?'

'It is now,' said Tom, and they all laughed, even Kate.

Then she said: 'Only, it's not funny, really. It's stealing.' And she held out her hand. 'Come on, Tom. Give it to me.'

But Tom kept hold of it. He folded it and

10

put it in his pocket. He turned his back to the sharp wind and wished he was still in the café. A paper bag cartwheeled along the path and wrapped and flapped around his ankles. He kicked it free and it flew on, towards a thin line of spectators watching a faraway football game. 'We didn't steal it,' he said quietly. 'We *found* it.'

'*We* found it? You mean *I* found it.'

Tom sneered. 'And that makes it all yours does it?'

'Yes.' Kate said. 'I mean, no. It's not any of ours. It's someone else's. But I found it, so I'm giving it back.'

Tom and Bee groaned, but Jas said: 'Kate's right. How would you like it if you lost all that money and some kids…?'

'Keep out of it, Jas,' Tom said. 'It's got nothing to do with you.'

'Yes it has. It's got as much to do with me as it has with you. I agree with Kate, we have to give it back.'

11

....

Thinking ahead

Trying to guess what will happen next is known as **predicting**. Predicting makes you think about the text as you read it, and gets you involved in the story. It doesn't matter if your predictions turn out to be right or wrong.

Use what you have discovered about Kate, Jas, Bee, and Tom to predict how the vote will turn out.

LOST AND FOUND

'Don't be stupid,' Tom said, and gave Jas a push in the chest with his free hand. 'How can you give it back when you don't even know whose it is?'

Jas spun around to face him. 'Do that again, and you'll be sorry.'

'Stop it!' said Kate. 'I don't believe this. We're supposed to be friends, aren't we.'

'Tell *him*. He started it.'

'I don't care who started it. We'll have a vote,' said Kate. 'Who says we give the money back?'

All mixed in

Although this extract of the story is mostly dialogue, there is narrative mixed in with it too. There is also some descriptive writing, telling the reader about the new setting for this part of the story.

Find some sentences or paragraphs in the extract which contain a lot of narrative.

Find some sentences or paragraphs which describe the new setting.

On with the Plot

While Tom was trying to persuade his friends that finding wasn't stealing, (and Kate was trying to persuade them that it was), Ben Horrocks was groping about on the floor under his seat at *Scoffalotti's*. Only what he was looking for wasn't there.

He should have guessed. Ernie and Rita had double-crossed him. They had promised Ben that his share from the robbery would be left under the seat in a brown envelope. But there was nothing there other than a puddle of sticky liquid, which was now smeared all over the sleeve of his expensive coat.

'What can I get you?' the waiter asked.

'Nothing,' snapped Ben, standing up and barging roughly past him on his way to the door. The waiter watched him go with a puzzled frown: it was the second time someone had stomped angrily away from that same table in the last half hour. Something very strange was going on.

Outside in the High Street, Ben found a

14

phone box. He dialled a number he knew by heart. Half a mile away, the mobile in Ernie Benson's pocket started to ring.

'What d'you mean, it isn't there? I left it exactly where I said… Like I told you: third table from the door… Of course I wouldn't lie to you…'

'Where has it gone, then?'

'I don't know,' Ernie said, 'but I'm beginning to have my suspicions.' He told Ben what they were. Then he added, slowly and coldly: 'Here's what we do. You go and guard the café: keep an eye on that waiter. Rita and I'll find those four kids. It shouldn't be difficult. I'm sure I saw them when we were driving home, down by the park.'

15

The story has moved, away from the children in the park and back to the café. A new character has appeared, too. And you, the reader, now know something the children don't know.

- Who is the new character?
- How does the waiter feel about him?
- Who are Ernie and Rita, and where have you met them before?
- What do you now know that the children don't know?

Plot

Plot is the name for the storyline. It is not the whole story, with all the details, descriptions, and dialogue. It is just the events and how they fit together. The plot of *Lost and Found* so far could be described like this:

> By chance, four children find some money under a chair in a high-street café. They take it to the park and argue about whether to keep it or not. What they don't know is that the money is a share-out after a robbery, and that soon the criminals will be looking for them.

This short description is called a **plot summary**. Summarising means picking out the main points and leaving out the detail.

Ups and downs

Stories don't give you the same feeling all the way through. Most stories have ups and downs.

For example: *Lost and Found* starts quietly with nothing much happening. Then Kate finds the envelope and everything changes. A big argument blows up between the friends. Ben's arrival brings danger too – danger the *reader* knows about but the friends don't.

As the old saying goes: *The plot thickens!*

The part of a plot where tension or danger begins to grow is known as a **build-up**. The high-point to which is it building is called the **climax**.

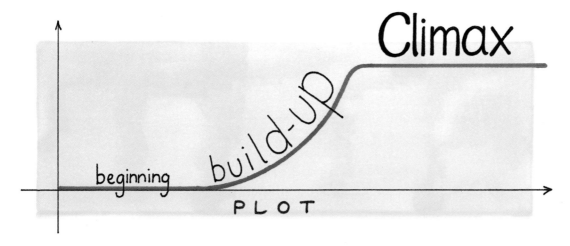

What do you predict the climax of *Lost and Found* will be?

On Stage and Screen

Not all texts are written to be read on the printed page. Some are written to be acted on stage, on film, or on television.

The next part of *Lost and Found* is written not as a narrative but as a piece of **drama**.

Scene 8 THE CAFÉ. WE SEE BEN ARGUING WITH THE WAITER, MARIO. WE CAN'T HEAR WHAT THEY ARE SAYING, BUT MARIO LOOKS SCARED.

Scene 9 LONG SHOT OF CHILDREN IN A GROUP, WALKING ALONG HIGH STREET. TOM IS STILL COMPLAINING.

TOM: This is stupid. Why are we going back to the café? What good is it going to do?

KATE: Don't start again, Tom. We had a vote, right? You lost. So we're taking the money back to the café, like we said we would.

TOM: No one lost. It was a draw. It was 2-2.

BEE: Yes, but then I changed my mind and that made it 3-1.

TOM: You can't change your mind *after* a vote.

JAS: 'Course you can. Your trouble is you're just a bad loser.

TOM: And you're just such a creep, you agree with anything Kate says.

KATE: (IGNORING THEM BOTH) We're giving the money to Mario. Then it's back where we found it. Where it should be. When the owner finds it's missing, they're sure to go there looking for… KATE GLANCES BEHIND HER AND STOPS IN MID-SENTENCE. THE OTHER THREE TURN AROUND TO SEE WHY, AND THE CAMERA SWINGS ROUND TO SHOW WHY: A CAR HAS PULLED UP AT THE ROADSIDE. RITA GETS OUT AND LEANS AGAINST IT. THERE IS A SOUR SMILE ON HER FACE. ERNIE CLIMBS OUT TOO AND STANDS BLOCKING THE PAVEMENT. HE HAS NO SMILE AT ALL.

BEE: I've got a nasty feeling that they already *have*.

Scripts

Drama is usually written as a **script** (short for **play-script** or **film-script** – also called a **screenplay**). The text you have just read is an extract from a script.

Scripts have two distinct parts:
directions, which set the scene and tell the actors what to do
lines, which tell the actors what to say/the words they will speak as characters.

Skips and jumps

Have you noticed that the story has 'skipped' forward in time since the four friends were last heard of? When we left them, they were about to vote about the money. Now they have voted.

From details in the script, what can you infer about what has happened in between?

When you read a script, you should try to imagine how it would look and sound if it was being performed. Better still, try acting it out in a group. You could try acting out Scenes 8 and 9.

Notice that in Scene 8 there are no *lines*, no spoken words, but the *directions* say that Mario looks scared.
Why do you think he is scared? Can you infer what Ben might be saying to him?

From the extract, can you tell which verb tense is always used for writing play-scripts? What are the reasons for this?

Stories can be told in the past tense or the present tense:
A car <u>pulled</u> up at the roadside... (past tense)
A car <u>pulls</u> up at the roadside... (present tense)

Hitting the Headlines

We've reached the climax of the plot, and also the ending of *Lost and Found*. The ending is told, not in ordinary narrative, but in the style of a newspaper story.

The Ditchford

We hear it, you read it

FAB FOUR FOIL P.O. ROBBERS

by Fred Fletcher

Two men and a woman were today charged with armed robbery from a small post-office, run by a couple in their sixties. Using toy guns, they forced them to open the safe, and escaped with thousands of pounds, in savings and pension money.

Police say they would probably have not been caught, except for the amazing courage and quick-thinking of four school children – Tom 10, Kate 11, Bee 9, and Jas 10. The four friends found the loot stashed under a seat in *Scoffalotti's* café, awaiting collection.

Echo

Monday 28 March

HIDE-OUT IN THE PARK

Taking the money with them, they cunningly went into hiding in a nearby park while the gang hunted them down, but were ambushed in the High Street as they tried to return to the café.

ARRESTED

A fierce scuffle followed, but *Scoffalotti's* waiter, Mario Marchi, who had earlier seen one of the gang acting very strangely, had already telephoned the police. They arrived before the thieves could snatch the money back, and arrested three people.

The honesty and bravery of the four young heroes earned them a big thank-you and a generous reward. ■

Newspaper story style

You can almost always recognize a newspaper story by its **style**. Style is not what a text is about, it is the way it is written or presented.

Newspaper stories have a very special style. They say things in a strong, punchy way, to make the reader interested. They have bold headlines and short paragraphs which get straight to the point, and little or no unnecessary detail.

Lost and Found, as we know, is a fictional story: it is made up. Real news stories belong to non-fiction. The events that they recount are facts, not inventions. The characters in them are real people, not fictional ones.

But beware...

Newspapers have to sell, and to get people to buy them, they have to gain the reader's interest. Sometimes, what you read in a newspaper has been made to sound more dramatic or more exciting or more dangerous than it really was. The reporter may make the bad characters sound really wicked; or the good characters nearly perfect.
This is called **exaggeration**.

Find three examples of exaggeration in the *FAB FOUR...* story.

Headlines are used a lot in newspapers. Like the stories themselves, headlines are meant to grab attention.
How do the headlines in the *FAB FOUR...* story help to grab attention?

What's What

Pure information

Fiction is written mainly to entertain readers. But there are many other kinds of text which are written to give readers information, add to their knowledge, or tell them what's what. Here is an example.

EATING OUT

Ditchford has many picturesque old houses lining its narrow, cobbled streets. In the centre there is an open-air market and an impressive town-hall, flanked by shops, restaurants and cafes. The newest is *Scoffalotti's*, a popular meeting place, especially with young people. For a more traditional atmosphere, there is the *Coach and Horses* and the *Old Bull Inn*...

This is the kind of text you would find in a **tourist guide**. The purpose is just to give information to visitors. It has a job to do. It doesn't have to be entertaining or exciting – and it isn't.

Information with a slant

Compare the tourist guide with this next text, which also gives information but in a very different way.

This text is an advert – or **advertisement**. What is its purpose? What is it saying and how does it say it? And in what ways is it different from the piece of tourist information?

One important difference is that the tourist guide is completely *factual*. The advertisement expresses *opinions* as well.

Scoff's, as the locals call it, is THE place to go.
Cheerful, friendly, fun to eat in, with great food and giant plates.
You bring your appetite, we do the rest. And it won't cost you a fortune either.

Fact or Opinion

Many texts are a mixture of facts and opinions. Opinions are statements that aren't true *or* false. Instead you either agree with them or you don't. You may *not* agree that the food in Scoff's is good, or that it's fun to be there – Ernie and Rita didn't think much of it.

It is very important to recognize which statements are given as facts in texts, and which are given as opinions.

Issues

Issues are subjects that we think, talk, or write about, and often disagree over. There is an important issue in *Lost and Found*, and it causes a big split between the four friends.

The issue is stealing, and whether keeping something that you find is the same as stealing. Is it just as bad as stealing?

The answer is a matter of opinion, not of fact. That is why there is a disagreement.

What is this next writer's opinion on the issue?

> If you find something valuable, and you know it belongs to someone else, it is wrong to keep it. It is obvious that it is wrong because you would not want someone else to do it to you: it would make you angry and upset. There is a golden rule that you should always treat others as you would like them to treat you. Therefore you should always give back anything that you find. Keeping it is as bad as stealing.

Arguments

There is something special about this piece of text. It is called an **argument.** It's not the kind of argument that Tom and Jas have: that's a quarrel. This is an argument which gives reasons which lead to a conclusion.

Arguments are mostly used to try to prove something, or show that it's right. (They don't always succeed, but that's the purpose.) The main point the argument is trying to make comes in the **conclusion**.

To understand an argument in a text, you have to be able to find its conclusion and the reasons that are given to support it.

What is the conclusion of the argument? Find three reasons given to support it.

For Information and Reference

We all need information. We need to know when buses and trains run, so we read **timetables**. We look at maps and **guide books** to help us find our way. We look in **encyclopedias** to find facts and in **dictionaries** to find meanings.

And we use computers to get information from databases or from the Internet.

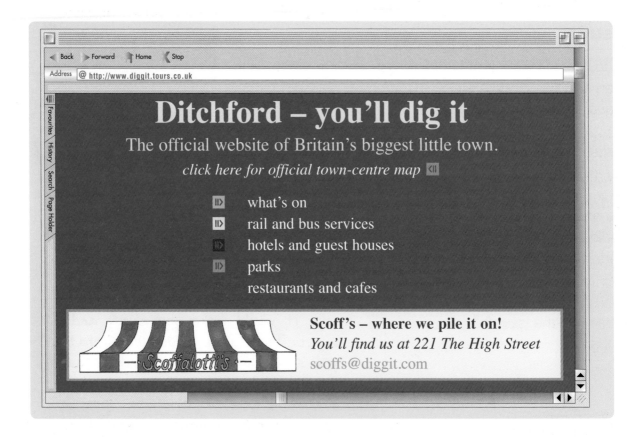

Texts like these are called **reference sources**. You *refer* to them to find things out. Usually they are organized in a special way to help your search. There may be key words you can look up in an index, or a contents page. Or the whole book may be in alphabetical order, like an encyclopedia.

What are the differences between the contents page, and the index? To make good use of reference books, it's important to learn to use these aids.
Refer to page 3 and pages 30–32, and use them to find some information about *dialogue*. Then try to find where *exaggeration* is talked about in this book.

Reading for information

When you read a text to get information, it is not the same as reading a story. You read a story from beginning to end. If you read the ending first, you can spoil the story for yourself. And a story may not make sense unless you read it from the beginning.

But when you read an information book, you may not want to learn about everything it contains. What you want to know may be scattered here and there in the book, and you need to know how to find it.

So two important skills to learn when you read for information are **skimming** and **scanning**.

In *skimming* you look quickly through the text, noting headings, and getting a general idea of what the text is about. Then when you read the text again more slowly, you know what to expect.

This helps with comprehension, because it gives you an outline of what you are going to read before you try to fill in the details. It is like doing a jigsaw. Once you have all the edges in place, it is much easier to fill in the middle part.

In *scanning* you are looking for particular pieces of information, that you may need for a piece of work, or to answer a question, without reading every word on every page. The idea is to let your eyes travel quickly through the text, looking for key words and phrases. It's like trying to find a very specific piece of a jigsaw.

Try skimming pages 26-29 and then stating, in one sentence, what you think they are *mainly* about. Then try scanning other parts of the book, to find some information about **narrative**, and about **plot**.

Not Literally

There is a wonderful poem that begins:

> This house has been far out at sea all night...

(You can read more from the poem on page 29.)

What does this first line mean? Does it mean that the poet's house was loaded on to a ship? Or that the tide came in and carried it away for the night?

No. That would be giving the words their literal meaning. **Literal** meaning is the meaning words normally have when stating facts or giving information.

But language has another, magical kind of meaning as well, that comes from using words to make pictures.

Imagine sitting all night in a house that is being battered by strong winds. It shakes and trembles like a ship at sea. That is what the poet is doing: he is *comparing* the experience of the storm to the experience of being at sea.

Two other words for a picture are 'image' and 'figure'. For that reason, language that creates a picture is called **figurative** (or a **figure of speech**). And the picture that the words make is called an **image**.

Turn to pages 30–32

Simile

A very common figure of speech is one called a **simile.** You can always recognize a simile as it uses the words *like* or *as* to make comparisons:

It shook and trembled <u>like</u> a ship at sea.
It felt <u>as</u> if the house was being tossed on the waves.

Metaphor

Another figurative use of language is **metaphor**. Metaphors also make comparisons, but not directly, like similes do. Metaphors leave the reader to make the comparison. The line from the poem we started with is a metaphor. It gives the reader an image of the house riding out the storm at sea as a ship does.

Can you think of some other comparisons for being in a wild storm?

Larger than life

A favourite figure of speech with many writers is deliberate exaggeration. Suppose you read the sentence:

The wind swept in from the sea at a million miles an hour.

You would understand that the writer was exaggerating, to create a picture of great speed. You would also realize, from this one clue, that the text it comes from is unlikely to be factual, or informative. It is more likely to be from a fictional story, or from a poem.

Deliberate exaggeration, that is not meant to be taken literally, is called **hyperbole** (which sounds like *hie-perbolly*) or **overstatement**. The opposite is **understatement**, for example, describing a violent storm as *a bit of a breeze*.

Always look out in your reading for non-literal uses of language. Comprehension often means looking beyond what words usually *mean*, to discover what they *suggest* to the reader.

Poetry

Poems need a very different kind of comprehension from factual or informative texts. For a start, they are much more likely to have figurative language in them, which can mean different things to different people.

In Ted Hughes' poem *Wind* on page 29, there is the line: *I scaled along the house-side.* Literally, *scaled* means climbed. But how can you *climb along* a house-side? What can this line mean?

The answer could be that the person is keeping so close to the wall, because of the storm, that it looks like he is climbing. This may not be the right, or the only answer, but it is a good answer because it explains that the writer does not mean the words literally, and suggests what they could mean instead. (The difference between figurative and literal language is explained on page 26.)

When you read a poem:
- *Don't* worry if you don't understand it all.
- *Do* read it carefully – more than once – and explore and question its meanings.

Find the line in which the hills are compared to a tent. In what way could hills be like a tent?
In verse 2, why do you think it says that *the hills had new places*? Wouldn't you say this was a bit of an exaggeration?
Find the two birds that are mentioned in the poem. How does Ted Hughes describe the difference in the way they are moving?

from **Wind**

This house has been far out at sea all night,
The woods crashing through darkness, the booming hills,
Winds stampeding the fields under the window
Floundering black astride and blinding wet.

Till day rose: then under an orange sky
The hills had new places, the wind wielded
Blade-light, luminous black and emerald,
Flexing like the lens of a mad eye.

At noon I scaled along the house-side as far as
The coal-house door. Once I looked up –
Through the brunt wind that dented the balls of my eyes
The tent of the hills drummed and strained its guy-ropes.

The fields quivering, the skyline a grimace,
At any second to bang and vanish with a flap:
The wind flung a magpie away and a black-
Back gull bent like an iron bar slowly…

Often poems have some unusual
words in them. You may need to
check on their normal meaning
in a dictionary. For example,
from this poem:
wield means swing something
   about like a sword
luminous means alight, glowing
flexing means bending, changing
   shape
guy-ropes are ropes used to
   support things – e.g. tents
grimace means a snarling face

Index

		page
advert	Short for **advertisement**, this is a text used to persuade people to buy something, or visit somewhere.	*22*
argument	An argument is a text which tries to persuade the reader or listener by giving reasons to support an opinion or idea.	*23*
audience	Whoever a text is *for* is called the 'audience', whether the text is printed, spoken, or performed.	*7*
autobiography	This is a text that tells someone's own life story and is written in the **first person**.	*8*
biography	Biography is the story of somebody's life and is written by another writer (in the **third person**).	*8*
build-up	This is the part of a story where excitement, tension, or interest grows. The build-up leads to a high point called the 'climax'.	*17*
character	Characters are the people in a story or play. Animals, and even machines, can be characters in some kinds of story.	*7, 12, 16*
climax	This is the high-point in a text, the most exciting or interesting part.	*17*
command	A command is a sentence which tells or instructs the audience to do (or not to do) something. Commands are also called 'imperatives'. Instruction texts usually contain a lot of imperative sentences.	*6*
comprehension	Understanding what you read or hear is called 'comprehension'.	*6*
conclusion	Conclusion has two meanings. It can just mean the end, or last part of a text. Or it can mean the main point in an argument.	*23*
dialogue	Dialogue means conversation or speech.	*14, 24*
diary	A diary is an account of someone's life, day to day, usually written in the first person.	*7*
dictionary	This is a reference book containing a long list of words in alphabetical order, with their meanings and uses explained.	*24*
directions	Directions are instructions. In drama texts the directions set the scene and tell the actors what to do.	*18*
drama	Play-scripts and film-scripts are drama texts.	*18*
encyclopedia	This is a reference book containing lots of short articles with the subjects arranged in alphabetical order.	*24*
events	These are the things that happen in a story.	*12*
exaggeration	Making something sound bigger, better, worse, more exciting, or more dramatic than it really is, is called exaggeration.	*21, 27, 28*
factual	Factual texts are accurate and true to real life.	*8, 22*
fiction	Fiction is any text which is made up by the speaker or writer.	*8*
figurative language	This means language that uses 'figures of speech'.	*26, 27, 28*
figure of speech	Something which is not meant literally, but is written to make a picture, or 'figure', in the mind.	*26*

Index

		page
first person	A text which tells something from the author's or a narrator's point of view, using *I*, *me*, and *we*, is said to be *in the first person*. (See **third person**).	**7**
genre	A genre is a kind of text. Some examples of different genres are: science fiction, romance, travel books, and newspaper stories.	**9**
glossary	A glossary is a list of words from a text which need explanation. What you are reading now is a glossary, as well as being an index. (See **index**).	**30-32**
headline	This is a word or phrase above the main part of a text, to catch the reader's interest. They appear in newspapers, magazines, Internet websites.	**20, 21**
hyperbole	It sounds like *hie-perbolly*, and means 'exaggeration' or 'overstatement'.	**27**
image	An image is a picture made by special uses of language (See **figurative language**.)	**26**
index	An index is an alphabetical list which tells you where to find things in a book by giving the page or chapter number. It is usually at the back of a book or in an appendix. This text is an index, as well as being a **glossary**.	**24, 30-32**
inference	Inference means working something out that is not stated in a text. If you read the sentence: *Tom was often rude to adults*, you could infer that Tom was a child, even though it doesn't say so in so many words.	**11**
information text	This is text which describes, explains, or lists, things.	**6, 22, 24, 25**
instructions	Instructions tell the reader or listener how to do something.	**6**
issue	An issue is an important subject that is discussed in a text. Often issues cause disagreement. A big issue discussed in this book is stealing.	**23**
lines	In a play-script or film-script, the lines are the words that the actors will speak.	**18, 19**
literal meaning	This is the meaning words normally have when they are used to state facts or give information.	**26**
metaphor	A metaphor makes a comparison, but without the use of the words *like* or *as*. For example: *Helga's temper boiled over*.	**27**
narrative	Narrative texts tell stories.	**7, 25**
narrator	A narrator is someone who tells a story. It might be one of the characters in a book or play or it might be the author's 'voice'. (See **voice**.)	**13**
non-fiction	Any text that is not fiction is called non-fiction.	**8**
novel	A novel is a fictional text that fills a whole book.	**8**
opinion	An opinion is something that the speaker or writer believes to be true or right.	**22**

Index

page

overstatement   This means exaggeration. (See **exaggeration**.)   *27*

plot   Plot means the storyline: the events in a story, and how they fit together.   *16, 17*

predicting   Predicting means guessing or working out what will come later on in a text or, more generally, in the future.   *14*

purpose   The purpose of a text is the reason why the author wrote it. For example, the purpose of a comedy is to make people laugh; the purpose of a recipe is to tell people how to cook a meal.   *4*

recounting   Recounting is to tell something that has happened.   *21*

reference text   This is text which stores information for the user to look up and find. Dictionaries, databases, and encyclopedias are examples of reference texts.   *24*

scanning   When you scan a text, you are looking for particular pieces of information that you may need for a piece of work or to answer a question, without reading every word on every page.   *25*

science fiction   Story texts set in the future or on other planets, or with imaginary technology, are called science fiction.   *9*

screenplay   This is a script written for a film. (See **script**.)   *18*

script   Short for **play-script** or **film-script**. It has lines for the actors to speak, and directions telling them what to do.   *18, 19*

setting   Where and when a story takes place is called its setting. The main story in this book is set in the town of Ditchford.   *12, 13*

simile   A simile is a comparison that is made by using the words *like* or *as*. For example, *Her temper was like a flash of lightning*.   *27*

skimming   When you skim, you look quickly through a text, noting headings, and getting a general idea of what the text is about.   *25*

slant   Texts which have a slant are one-sided in what they say. They don't try to give a balanced or a fair picture. Another word for slant is 'bias'.   *22*

style   The style of a text is the way it is written and presented, not what it is about.   *21*

summary   In a summary you pick out the main points and leave out the detail.   *17*

text   A text can be anything that is written, or spoken out loud.   *4*

third person   Third person texts are about other people, rather than being about the author or narrator. (See **first person**.)   *7*

tourist guide   This is a book, leaflet, or website giving information to visitors about the place they are visiting.   *22*

understatement   This is the opposite of **overstatement**. Describing a big meal as *a bite to eat* is understatement.   *27*

voice   The person the author chooses to tell a story is known as the 'voice'. It might be the author's own voice, or the voice of one of the characters.   *13*